905-780-0711

Fast Slide

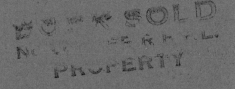

Fast Slide

Melanie Jackson

Orca currents

ORCA BOOK PUBLISHERS

Library and Archives Canada Cataloguing in Publication

Jackson, Melanie, 1956-
Fast slide / written by Melanie Jackson.
(Orca currents)

Issued also in an electronic format.
ISBN 978-1-55469-343-6 (bound).--ISBN 978-1-55469-342-9 (pbk.)

I. Title. II. Series: Orca currents
PS8569.A265F38 2010   jC813'.6   C2010-903581-X

First published in the United States, 2010
Library of Congress Control Number: 2010929087

Summary: Clay Gibson, teen lifeguard, has to solve the mystery
of the emptied register.

Mixed Sources
Cert no. SW-COC-001271
© 1996 FSC

FSC

*Orca Book Publishers is dedicated to preserving the environment and has printed
this book on paper certified by the Forest Stewardship Council.*

Orca Book Publishers gratefully acknowledges the support for its publishing
programs provided by the following agencies: the Government of Canada
through the Canada Book Fund and the Canada Council for the Arts,
and the Province of British Columbia through the BC Arts Council
and the Book Publishing Tax Credit.

Cover design by Teresa Bubela
Cover photography by Getty Images

ORCA BOOK PUBLISHERS
PO Box 5626, Stn. B
Victoria, BC Canada
V8R 6S4

ORCA BOOK PUBLISHERS
PO Box 468
Custer, WA USA
98240-0468

www.orcabook.com
Printed and bound in Canada.

14 13 12 11 • 4 3 2 1

To the other Melanie J.—my editor,
Melanie Jeffs—with appreciation.

Chapter One

Her fingers dug into my arm.

"Come on, Clay. Say we'll take lunch break together. *Please*?"

I shook her hand off. I tried to keep the impatience out of my voice. "No, Aggie. You're nice and all, but I don't want to have lunch with you. Now get lost."

Aggie stared at me with her pale gray eyes. Everything about her was pale: her bleached hair, her skin, her lips.

Aggie Wentworth was a summer employee at North Vancouver's new jungle-themed water park, Safari Splash. She was a cashier in the souvenir shop.

I was a lifeguard at the Boa, a two-hundred-thirty-foot waterslide that twisted down Grouse Mountain. The Boa was the most popular ride at Safari Splash. It was the fastest—and the loudest. The tube was like an echo chamber. It amplified every crash of the rubber rafts against the tube wall. Also, every scream and every sound of the passengers, including the occasional cuss word.

The noise only made the Boa more appealing. People who had come to the park planning to try only the easy rides would hear it and decide they couldn't miss out on the excitement.

My job was to make sure every passenger got out of their raft and safely onto the landing platform. After churning around inside the Boa for the fast winding drop, passengers were dizzy. Left on their own, they might topple into the landing pool.

The end of the tube was like a Boa's mouth, complete with fangs hanging down. It was corny, but people loved it. They snapped up the *I rode the Boa!* T-shirts at the souvenir shop.

Boa guard—a dignified start to my résumé. I'd wanted to be an apprentice lifeguard at Kits Beach. My swimming medals and my Royal Lifesaving Society certificate were enough to get me a job there.

But Mom insisted I take this job. She and Dad were friends with the owner, Bill Costello. In vain I'd argued, yelled, sulked. So, here I was, stuck hanging out at the landing platform with Aggie.

Aggie giggled. "I like your intense routine, Clay: that fierce scowl, those smoldering blue eyes…"

That made me laugh. It was too true. I curved my fingers into claw shapes and growled at Aggie. She was fun. At least she had been till she got clingy.

The first couple of days here, I hadn't objected when Aggie tagged along with me at breaks. I was glad to meet her. I didn't know any of the other kids. They all lived near the water park and went to the same school. I was the stranger. But then Aggie began glomming on to me. I couldn't shake her. It was like I'd become her obsession.

With the back of her hand, Aggie wiped a band of sweat off her upper lip. Her pale eyes studied me, worried. "That growling thing you did just now. Was that a lynx imitation? Were you making fun of lynx?"

This was so left field, I just stared at her.

Aggie confided, "I'm afraid of lynx."

She glanced around the park, and then I got it. The Lynx was a ride at Safari Splash. The slide was fairly tame. It was only a triple spiral before splashdown.

I laughed at her. "Lynx is nothing. It's Boa that's the safety hazard."

We'd had to close the Boa briefly last week after someone hit their head against the tube wall. It was some idiot not obeying the rules. He took off his safety belt. When the Boa reopened, it was even more popular than before. People loved the idea of risk.

Aggie shook her head. She was gripping my arm again. "I'm not kidding, Clay. Lynx is dangerous."

I tried to pull away. She raised her voice. "Please don't ignore me, Clay."

People were pausing to stare. I knew what Aggie was up to. She was trying to embarrass me into agreeing to hang out with her at lunch.

Through the waterslide tube, I heard passenger screams. I heard the raft crashing against the Boa's sharp twists. Soon the raft would slam into the landing pool.

Prying Aggie's arm loose, I pushed her away. I didn't shove all that hard, but she staggered and fell on the platform.

She lay there, not moving.

"Aggie…*Aggie*…," I said.

With a moan, Aggie sat up. She rubbed the elbow she'd smashed against the platform.

"I'm really sorry," I said, helping her to stand. "I just need to be on my own for a while. I never meant to knock you down." Privately, I wondered if I should start wearing a *Danger: Do Not Approach* sign. My folks kept urging me to curb my temper. They had a point.

Aggie's elbow was bloody.

I said, "We'd better get you to the Red Cross station." There was one behind the office. I could signal Judd, the guard at the top of the Boa, to halt the rides till I got back. People in line would be mad, but they could work on their tans.

Aggie shook her head. Her eyes got kind of buggy. I didn't get it.

I didn't have time to think about it. The giant tube winding down the Mountain shuddered with the force of the raft inside.

"We'd better move," I warned Aggie.

I jumped out of the way. I could have pulled her with me, but I was afraid to touch her. She seemed easy to damage.

Wham. The raft crashed into the pool. A gigantic wave rose like a hand to slap down on Aggie.

The people watching from below frowned at me. I bet they blamed me for Aggie's dousing.

I threw Aggie a towel from the stack we kept for people getting off the ride.

Aggie was looking around like she expected to see someone.

I looked around too. I saw what I always saw. Below us was the Ruby Parrot, a short waterslide for kids. It had lots of squawking sound effects. The Lynx, beside it, was one age level up from the Parrot. The Safari Splash office was farther downhill. Beside the office was the Starfish Souvenir Shop, with its tacky T-shirts and plastic jewelry. That place was sucker heaven.

On either side of Safari Splash were the slopes of Grouse Mountain, the Douglas firs a vivid blue-green in the bright sun.

Who, or what, was Aggie looking for?

I turned to help two teenage couples onto the platform. Three of them were laughing and shaking water loose from their hair. The fourth, a guy with a buzz cut, was greenish, like he was ready to throw up.

I thought again about how I could have been an apprentice lifeguard at Kits Beach. There would be sun, surf, pretty girls needing resuscitation. At least, that was what I imagined.

"Clay, how much do you know about Lynx?"

The only girl paying attention to me at Safari Splash was this pale clingy one.

"Get over it," I snapped. "It's just a ride."

At the top of the Boa, Judd was sending a raft with a fresh round of passengers into the tube. I heard squeals as it bashed into the first turn. The echo-chamber effect was so distinct, I also heard the passengers' every word.

"I LOVE YOU, HENRY!"

"SO MARRY ME, ALICE!"

Henry and Alice didn't realize how clearly their voices carried. A waterslide.

What a stupid place to launch a marriage, I thought.

But then, I was cranky.

I warned Aggie, "You're gonna get clobbered by another wave."

Aggie's eyes took on a sharpness, an acceptance. "All right, Clay. I'm through bothering you. I do like you though. You're a good guy. It's a shame."

She looked feverish. Red splotches stood out against her pale skin. That's why she was blathering nonsense, I thought. She was sick.

"Aggie, you gotta go home. I'll tell Mr. Costello you don't feel well."

She shook her head, like I'd got the wrong answer.

She glanced around the park yet again. This time her gaze came to rest on Judd, at the top of the Boa.

She turned to walk away—but not before I saw the glint of fear in her eyes.

Chapter Two

The Boa shook violently. The next instant, it spewed out another squealing group. Everyone was laughing except for an old lady holding her hand over her mouth.

I grabbed a barf bag from beside the towels and held it out to the lady. Warnings posted at the Boa included cautions against older people taking the ride.

It took five seconds to stop and read the warnings. Why didn't people bother?

Instead of taking the barf bag, the old woman leaned over and heaved right into the pool.

Now I had to close the Boa to scoop out her barf.

I waved my arms at Judd to signal that he shouldn't let another raft go.

I also wanted to ask Judd why Aggie was afraid of him. But that would have to wait.

I helped the old lady and the other passengers out of the raft. I managed— just barely—to give them a cheerful Safari-Splash smile.

Then I started scooping out the old lady's barf.

"Hi, Clay. How's it going?"

Bradley Costello, the owner's son, was standing on the platform, watching me through his black-framed glasses. Wiping a Kleenex over his sweaty forehead,

Brad managed to knock the glasses crooked. Before he could catch them, they tumbled to the platform.

It was a classic dorky Bradley moment. I felt like pointing out that Brad wouldn't sweat so much if he didn't wear a suit. A silk suit, yet.

Brad had a job in the office. *Helping out*. Right. He surfed the Net while the rest of us, stuck in moronic camouflage-style uniforms, had to do actual work.

Since Brad and I were toddlers, my parents had tried to get me to hang out with him. Mom, especially. She was always saying it wasn't his fault he was bookish.

Bookish? Try encyclopedic. Our families' get-togethers were painful. At dinner Brad would fidget and blurt out factoids with a high-pitched laugh, trying to impress everyone. One day it would be weather patterns. The next visit it was economics or mountains in Peru.

We learned every useless detail about whatever he happened to be into.

The irony was, I did make friends with a Costello—just not Brad. I liked talking to his dad. Mr. Costello had been a swim champion at college. His trophies lined the hallway of his house, shining like the Milky Way. Mr. Costello had inspired me to take swimming seriously. The Costellos had a pool out back, and he'd noticed me plowing up and down in power laps.

You've got a gift, Clay, he told me. *You're a natural. But being a natural isn't enough. When you've got a gift, you've gotta work at it. It's like a duty.*

I'd told him that I loved swimming. I loved the clean way you felt when you moved through the water. It was like flying.

That conversation meant a lot to me, even though Brad almost ruined it by spouting out some factoid about the history of swimming pools.

My approach was to avoid Brad or suffer death by boredom. Luckily, like the other kids working at Safari Splash, he lived around here. I didn't have to endure him at my own school.

"How's it going?" he repeated.

"How do you think it's going?" I snapped. "I'm cleaning up some old lady's barf. Wanna help?"

I was being sarcastic, but Brad dropped to his knees beside me.

"Okay," he said. He picked up a spare scooper.

I felt bad. I'd been rude to him, and he was being decent.

Brad flailed the scooper at the water. The guy was as clumsy as a blind baboon.

"Hey," I said uneasily. "You're leaning kind of far—"

SPLASH!

Bradley Costello didn't have a clue how to swim. He was afraid of the water.

Kicking off my sneakers, I got ready to dive in. My day was getting better and better.

I looked up to the top of the slide to see if Judd knew Brad was in the water. Judd was talking to Aggie. She pointed down at me and shook her head. I could tell she was upset.

I didn't have time to wonder about it. *Bradley* needed rescuing.

"Gee, thanks, Clay." Brad was trying to squeeze water out of his jacket sleeve without taking off the jacket. The guy was clueless. "I was trying to help, not screw up."

I didn't trust myself to reply.

We were in the control room. I was changing into a dry uniform—there were spares for an event like this. A lifesaving. Except this was a *dork*saving.

Brad interrupted my thoughts. "I sure hope Dad isn't watching. He'll rip into me for being clumsy."

I guess Brad had his problems.

I squinted out the control-room door to the top of the Boa. I was curious about Aggie. I was troubled by how agitated she'd looked.

Judd was on his own again. He wasn't smiling and chatting up the passengers like a good Safari Splash employee, though. He was standing at the edge of the platform, staring darkly into the Douglas firs.

I interrupted Brad, who was yakking about how much his suit had cost. "Tell me about Aggie Wentworth."

Brad stared owlishly at me.

Earth to Brad. You go to school with these kids. "The pale blond who works in the souvenir shop. She seems scared about something."

Brad bobbed his head. "Sure, I know Aggie. I haven't paid a whole lot of attention to her."

That's because you're off on Planet Bradley all the time, I thought.

"Why would Aggie be scared?" he asked.

I hesitated. Brad was spacey, but bright. He might be able to help. "Aggie made a strange comment. She asked me if I knew about the Lynx."

Brad's eyes widened. "The *Lynx*?" He seemed at a loss for words. "You mean the waterslide?"

"Yeah, it's crazy," I agreed. "A tame slide like that." I shrugged. "I've been wondering if she meant something else."

Brad flapped at his lips with a forefinger. "Maybe she's afraid of lynxes. She might have seen one. Generally, lynxes prefer deep forests, away from coastal areas. One *could* have ventured down here though."

"Yeah, maybe."

I didn't think Brad was right. I didn't think Aggie had meant a stray animal. Still, Brad had tried to help me. For a dork, he could be okay sometimes.

And other times he was just as dorky as always.

After a trip home to change into a fresh suit, Brad returned to the Boa. "Sorry about the trouble I caused. It won't happen again, I promise." He leaned on the large wheel at the center of the control panel.

"Hey, stay away from that!" I said.

At my sharp tone, Brad sprang off— like a frightened grasshopper, I thought. "Sorry, Brad," I said, "but I can't risk you budging the wheel even slightly."

"Why?" asked Brad.

"It controls the Boa's water flow. For rides, we keep the wheel where it is now.

Turning the wheel more would produce too much water—riders and rafts would be submerged."

"Why not keep the water constant?" Brad asked.

"We increase the water pressure to clean the pool," I explained.

Brad studied a digital clock showing red zeroes. "What's this for?"

"It's a timer," I said. "We could set the wheel to turn automatically for the end-of-day tube cleaning. But, with the long lineups we're getting, we never know for sure when the Boa will close."

Brad's eyes popped. He let out an ear-splitting yell.

I turned. A broad-shouldered figure was pressed against the control-room window. The figure was wearing a camouflage uniform. It was another Safari Splash employee.

With one difference.

He had the head of a lynx.

Chapter Three

A chill went through me—for a nanomoment. It wasn't a lynx head, but a lynx face mask: teeth bared, incisors gleaming, eyes fiery.

It was a cheap mask and a cheap trick to scare us. "It's okay," I told Brad.

The lynx face dropped away. I unlocked the window, pushed it wide and looked around.

I saw a flash of green and beige around a twist of the tube. Our trickster was climbing to the top of the Boa.

The figure was the right height and build to be Judd. I looked to top of the Boa. When on duty, Judd was supposed to be on his platform at all times.

He wasn't now.

Back in the control room, Brad was waiting for me. He managed a smile, sort of. "Sorry you had to be part of that, Clay. This is just another practical joke. They have been happening since the park opened. One time someone left glue on my chair. I've had my lunch stolen from the office fridge. Whoever it was left stones in my lunch bag instead."

What Brad had just described was bullying. And bullies preyed on people who scared easily.

"Judd's your practical joker," I said. I remembered how upset Aggie had looked when she was with Judd on the launch platform. "And Judd is Aggie's lynx. Maybe he's been bullying her too."

It was an effort to keep my voice calm, not to upset Brad. I didn't feel calm. I felt like marching up to the top of the ride and shoving that mask down Judd's throat.

Mr. Costello relieved me for my half-hour lunch break. Usually the owner's face brightened when saw me. This time he just looked worried. "What's this I hear about you having a violent argument with Aggie Wentworth? I'm told you knocked her to the ground."

"I wasn't violent, Mr. C.," I said. "I pushed Aggie away because she was clinging to my arm. She wouldn't let go."

"Well, now Aggie's walked out. She didn't even say anything. She just left."

I stared at him. I wondered if Aggie had bolted Safari Splash because of Judd. What had he said to her?

Mr. Costello gave me a tired grin. "I take it Aggie has a crush on you, Clay. No surprise there." He ruffled my hair. "My Janice thinks you're something too."

Janice was his daughter, Brad's twin sister. I hadn't seen Janice for almost a year. I bet she wouldn't be too pleased with her dad for telling me this. I grinned, embarrassed.

Mr. Costello shrugged. "Well, if Aggie can't take rejection, too bad. But go easy on the temper, Clay."

I shook my head. "It's not my temper Aggie's scared of. It's the lynx, aka—"

Judd, I was going to say, but Mr. Costello interrupted. "Aggie's afraid of the Lynx waterslide?" he scoffed. "If anything, we should ramp it up. We've only got one scary ride, and that's what people are coming for."

Through the Boa's mouth echoed half-panicked, half-laughing yells. Mr. Costello beamed. "Those screams are my ka-chings!"

Usually on my break I headed over to Safari Sizzle, the water park's outdoor restaurant. Under one of the plastic palm trees, I'd guzzle an iced coffee. The stronger the caffeine hit, the better, since my job was so dull.

Today I didn't need the caffeine hit. I was already buzzed. I wanted to confront Judd. "Excuse me," I said, edging past the crowd on the Boa stairs.

Giggles from a bunch of girls. Preteen girls—the worst kind.

They pretended to swoon. "Oooooo, *hi*. Bump against us anytime."

"Only if I'm armed with a can of Raid," I retorted.

At the top of the stairs, the next people in line for a raft waited behind a line painted like a—you guessed it—

boa constrictor. On either side of the painted line were two metal posts. I stretched the chain from one post and fastened it to a hook on the other.

Ignoring the protests that erupted, I shouted at Judd, "We need to talk. Now."

Till now, Judd and I had gotten along well enough. Now he was scowling. "Beat it, Gibson."

Grabbing his arm, I tried to pull Judd behind the bamboo screen into the storage area. "What's the idea?"Judd asked as he wrenched his arm free.

"I want a word," I said. "In private."

Judd crossed his arms. He wasn't going to budge.

People in line were gaping at us. "If you want to make this public, fine," I snapped. I placed a palm on Judd's chest and shoved him against the wall. "Listen and learn. Only losers hide behind masks."

"Dunno what you're talking about."

He was lying. I could tell by the way his small, dark eyes skittered from side to side.

"What did you say to Aggie?" I demanded. "After you gave the poor kid the full force of your charm, she walked out."

"Oh, I get it. Our resident champion blunders in to save the day," jeered Judd. "You should stick to blowing bubbles, Gibson."

All this time, his dark eyes kept skittering.

I twisted his shirt and shoved him harder against the wall. "What's with the lynx routine? *What did you say to Aggie?*"

"Do we get our ride or not?" someone called.

An older guy ducked under the chain. "C'mon, boys, break this up."

I had to let Judd go. Able to relax now, he smirked at me. In a low voice, he taunted, "Lemme tell you about lynxes. They're in control at all times. And they toy with their prey before destroying it. *Just like I'm toying with you.*"

In my opinion, Judd needed a sock to the jaw—but the Boa-goers wanted their ride. I stomped down the stairs. High-pitched giggles greeted me. "Hi, Clay," cooed one of the girls. "Will you rescue me if I fall in the landing pool?"

"Unlikely," I snapped, brushing past. I was bracing myself to meet Mr. Costello. He had to have noticed the delay with the raft. He must have seen me arguing with Judd, right after he'd asked me to cool my temper.

But when I reached the lower platform, Mr. Costello wasn't there. In his place was a tall girl with long reddish brown hair and green eyes. "Hi, Clay."

It took me a moment to recognize her. "Janice?" I asked. The last time I'd seen Brad's sister, she'd been knobby-kneed and skinny, her teeth a silver sheen of braces.

"Dad was called to the souvenir shop. He asked me to stand in."

I realized I was staring. We were in a water park full of fake palms and fake grass roofs, and the most beautiful natural green was in this girl's eyes.

WHISH! The next raft spun out of Boa's mouth, landing with a sideways splash that tossed a blanket of water right over me. Janice, who'd stepped back, laughed.

"Smooth one, Clay."

"C'mon," I objected, shaking my arms free of water. "I was distracted."

"Yeah? By what?"

"By you," I said and grinned at her.

But Janice didn't hear. Her smile had faded. She was looking past me in concern.

Mr. Costello was running toward us. His face was gray, like he'd aged forty years.

Charging up the platform steps, the water park owner panted, "*Clay*. When Aggie left, did she tell you where she was going? Or why?"

I shook my head. Mr. Costello leaned against the landing-pool wall. He breathed raggedly, not like a trained swimmer at all.

"With Aggie gone, I had to take over the cash register in the souvenir shop. *The register was empty*. Cleaned out."

Chapter Four

Aggie had looked scared.

Because she'd just lifted the contents of the cash register?

I hadn't thought Aggie was dishonest. Clingy, yes. A thief, no.

Janice was having the same doubts. "You think *Aggie Wentworth* stole the money? I dunno, Dad. I've known Aggie since elementary school. I can't see it."

"Who else could it be?" Mr. Costello asked. "Other cashiers can open the register. But this one has built-in storage under the drawer. You need a personal identification number to open it. And only Aggie and I know the PIN."

I remembered how Aggie kept glancing around the park. I still didn't think she was a thief—but maybe she knew something. Maybe she knew who the thief was.

That would explain her nervousness. She knew too much for her own good.

"Last time I saw Aggie, it seemed like she thought someone was after her," I said.

Mr. Costello's mouth clamped in a grim line. "She'll have people after her, all right: the Police Department. I've just called them. They're sending a detective over."

The water park owner's face crumpled. He was near tears. "How could this happen?"

Janice put an arm around her dad's shoulders. "It's just a half-day's take, Dad. It's not like she made off with the contents of the office safe."

In response, Mr. Costello fixed haunted eyes on her. "Janny, you know I hate that safe. I can never remember the combination, and half the time the door sticks. Every night, I empty all the park's money and receipts into the till drawer.

"It had a week's worth of cash. Almost forty thousand dollars."

Mr. Costello's cell phone rang. He listened, then flipped it shut. "The police are waiting in the office. This is my fault. I should have put the money in the bank every day. I was so busy worrying about *making* money that I forgot about keeping it safe."

He clapped me on the shoulder. "You're doing a great job, Clay. Just keep the Boa going, and don't let this get to you."

But it had already gotten to me, big-time. I couldn't get Aggie's frightened face out of my mind.

Mr. Costello waved at Judd to let the next raft go. Then he strode away, Janice hurrying after him.

"Help! Help me, Clay!"

I'd been staring toward the office, where the police were questioning Mr. Costello. I wrenched my gaze back to the landing pool. "*Aggie?*"

But it was those moronic girls, giggling at me from a raft.

"You need help, all right," I growled. "*Mental* help."

This just set them off more. They headed straight back to the Boa lineup. Great. First Aggie, now them. Why did I attract the goofballs?

Janice wasn't a goofball though. With Janice around, working here was worthwhile. Someday, when this robbery stuff was cleared up, I'd like to explain to Janice how distracting I found her. I grinned at the thought—and an elderly couple walking by beamed at me.

My good humor was short-lived though. I thought about Aggie again. If she was involved in the theft, someone had forced her into it. And I was pretty sure I knew who.

Lemme tell you about lynxes, Judd had boasted. *They're in control at all times*.

Judd, I thought. Judd had masterminded the robbery.

I wanted to march right up to the launch platform and have it out with him. Really have it out, this time. Pound it out of him—

Calm down, Clay. This is exactly what gets you into trouble.

In any case, I couldn't stop the ride yet again for another confrontation.

I heaved deep breaths. Mom thought this job, with meeting the public all day, would make me more tolerant. I could at least *try*. I managed to smile at the next rafters who splashed down—even though I'd heard their complaints loud and clear through the tube. Seems the chlorine level was too high for them.

The sun rose higher and burned in the sky. More and more people lined up for the Boa. Forget the thrills. They just wanted a refreshing soak. Some show-offy college kids dove off the raft into the landing pool. I was too hot, too preoccupied with the robbery to tell them off.

"Clay, Clay—!"

The gigglers again.

"Give it a break," I snapped.

Then I saw that one of them was in the water. She wasn't giggling. She was choking. Her arms flailed—and she sank.

Jeez, I hadn't even been watching. I dove in, grabbing her under the chin. Using my free arm, I plowed to the pool steps. I dragged her onto the platform.

She wasn't breathing.

I pressed my hands on her chest to force the water out of her lungs.

Come on, I thought. Come on…

One of her eyes opened. Her braces glinted. A sly smile flashed over her face.

She was faking.

Furious, I jumped up. I let loose my bottled-up rage about Judd. I yelled, "You think drowning is *funny*, moron? What's next, you set yourself on fire for laughs? Harness your braces to a moving train? You are such a LOSER."

The girl's face was crumpling, but I was too mad to care, too out of control. I blasted on.

"Next time you set one fat foot in this water park, I'll have you thrown out.

No, better. I'll throw you out myself, down the rocky hill."

The day ticked along. I noticed fewer people laughing. Some stared at me. Maybe they'd heard my outburst at the giggler. Or maybe it wasn't that at all. Maybe people sensed the unease that had crept like a fog into the water park. There was a feeling of something gone very, very wrong.

Finally I couldn't stand it anymore. I grabbed the phone linking the landing pool with the top of the ride.

"Yeah?" Judd barked.

"Aggie's getting blamed for the robbery," I said.

"What robbery?"

In theory, Judd wouldn't have heard about the robbery. But his tone just now, his pretend ignorance, was as phony as the plastic Boa mouth.

"You were in on it, Judd. I think you planned it," I said. "The police are in Mr. Costello's office. If you're smart, you'll go talk to them before they come after you."

"I dunno anything about a robbery. Oh, wait, yeah, I do know something."

"What?" I asked.

"I know that it's fun watching you squirm, champ."

Judd pushed off another raft. A fresh round of yells echoed through the Boa's mouth.

Judd was messing with me. Again, my impulse was to throttle the guy.

I had to calm down. My coach always said not to panic in a crisis. Stop, rest and think. Cool your brain off so it can work again.

Think.

Okay, I told myself. There's been

a robbery. Aggie's the suspect. Judd's involved up to his skittering eyeballs.

Confronting Judd was useless. He'd just jeer at me with cryptic remarks about a lynx. That wasn't proof. I couldn't take that to the police.

All I could do was tell them about Aggie being scared of someone called the Lynx.

Wait a minute. *Lynx*. The lynx *mask*. In my mind, I saw the leering plastic fangs as Judd spied on Brad and me through the control-room window.

The mask would have Judd's fingerprints—heck, his *face* prints— on it.

The mask would be proof that Judd was Aggie's Lynx.

I needed to get the mask—but how?

Judd had been wearing it when he scrambled up Grouse to the top of the Boa. When I'd tried to drag Judd behind the bamboo screen later, he'd resisted.

He didn't want me to see behind the screen—*because that's where he'd stashed the mask.*

Chapter Five

I punched in the office number.

"Safari Splash." Janice sounded anxious.

"It's Clay. How's it going with the police? Have they found Aggie?"

Janice faded her voice to a whisper. "No. They've been to Aggie's house, but she's not there. Her parents don't know anything. But this detective who's here now, Detective Mulligan—"

"Mulligan? Like the stew?" I said.

"It's not funny, Clay. Detective Mulligan is horrible. He says Dad could have stolen the money himself. Brad's near tears, which only puts Dad more on edge. My poor bro isn't very good at coping."

"How could your dad be a suspect? *It's his money!*"

"Detective Mulligan says owners sometimes steal from their companies, then file an insurance claim. It's a way of doubling profits."

"Like your dad would do that," I said in disgust.

I thought of Brad, worried and upset, annoying his dad without meaning to.

I said, "Hey, Janice? Let's get Brad out of wrath range. Send him over here. I've got something for him to do."

At the end of every day, I stopped water flowing through the pipes into the launch pool. I drained both launch and landing pools. Once they were empty, I turned the water-control wheel on full blast. At the top of the ride, Judd poured in cleanser.

It was the shock-and-awe approach to sanitation. The sudsy blast flushed out every flip-flop that had come loose on the wild ride, every food wrapper, every wad of gum that some jerk had spat into the foam. The Boa belched it all into the landing pool. Then I had to drain the pool and scoop up all the garbage.

While the Boa was being cleaned, Judd walked down the sandy path underneath to check for cracks or dents in the tube.

It took Judd about twenty minutes to descend the length of the tube and then climb back up.

In those twenty minutes, I was going to hunt for the mask.

Brad's eyes widened behind his thick glasses when I told him my plan. "I dunno if Mulligan would approve. He might start yelling."

"Mulligan won't yell once he realizes the mask's significance. The mask connects Judd to Aggie. This is where you come in, Brad. You can help me."

Brad nodded. He wiped a tissue over his forehead.

I led Brad into the control room, where I twisted the wheel all the way to the right.

"All you have to do is guard the landing pool till I get back. The park's closed, but people hang around. Make sure no hotshots dive in while the water's flooding down and no little kids toddle up and fall in."

Brad looked nervous, and, in a shy way, pleased. "I'll stand guard, Clay. I won't let you down."

I clapped him on the shoulder. "If I'm not back in twenty, turn the wheel off. After that point, water will overflow into the drains. That'll mean a lot more cleanup, plus it'd be a huge waste of water."

I stepped out of the control room. I watched Judd pour cleanser into the launching pool, then jump down to the path under the tube. He was starting his inspection.

Still, I hesitated. I was asking a lot of Brad. I might get him into trouble. "Are you sure you're okay with this? I'm breaking the rules by leaving my post."

He managed a wobbly grin. "Don't worry. I'm okay."

"Good guy."

I started outside the control-room window where Judd, wearing his lynx mask, had spied on Brad and me.

From there it was an easy jump to the fir-needle-carpeted slope.

As water thundered down through the tube, I jogged up the slope, breathing in the scent of the Douglas firs.

At some point I would come parallel with Judd as he worked his way down. About halfway up, I slowed. I walked carefully, squinting deep into the trees as I looked for him.

Then—

Through the firs, I saw Judd. Head tipped back, he was examining the tube.

His cell phone rang, startling both of us.

Pulling the phone out of a back pocket, Judd barked, "Yeah?"

This was a chance to edge past Judd, up the slope, but his next words arrested me.

"Huh?…*Aggie?*…You're at the top *again*? But that wasn't the plan. I thought you were going to…Yeah, okay.

I get it, Aggie. Or should that be, *Naggie*? Nag, nag, nag."

Aggie was at the top of the ride.

Judd said, "Sure, everything's under control. I'll see you once I finish checking the Boa. My *last* check, I'm happy to say. No more Boa for this boy. A Lynx triumph!" He snickered.

Yeah, everything's under control—if you're a thief, I thought. But I'm going to reach Aggie before you do. Whatever Aggie's done, I'll convince her to come clean with Mr. Costello.

Judd snickered some more into the phone, calling her Naggie again. I tiptoed past Judd and ran the rest of the way.

I glanced around the launch platform. The water rushing into the pool gleamed diamond-bright in the slanting sun. Soon this part of the mountain would be shady.

I stepped behind the bamboo screen. Just the usual stuff there—cleanser, locker, towels, hamper, freezer, Red Cross kit.

No sign of Aggie.

I felt Aggie's presence though. I could see her face, pale and pleading. *Please, Clay*...I could feel her need for help. Maybe that's why she'd been so clingy earlier. She'd been guilty and frightened about her part in the robbery.

Maybe Aggie had spotted me approaching. She might be hiding. "I'm on your side," I called.

I surveyed the forest, but no answer came back. The sun was disappearing. The firs were inking together, turning the mountain black.

I had the peculiar sensation of not being alone, and yet being very, very alone.

And in danger. I had a strong urge to scramble back down the hill.

But I had to find the mask.

And maybe, while I was looking, Aggie would muster the nerve to come forward.

I opened the locker. Judd's knapsack lay inside. I had a qualm about going into someone else's belongings. It was the same as trespassing.

But Judd hadn't felt any qualms about ripping off Mr. Costello.

I reached for the knapsack.

Then I saw I didn't need to trespass, after all. Behind the knapsack, jammed in a locker, was the lynx mask.

I grabbed it by the tip. I'd watched enough cop shows to know about preserving fingerprints.

Water stopped gushing out of the pipes. It had been twenty minutes. Brad had kept his word and shut it off.

In the sudden quiet, I heard a breeze whistle through the firs. Or was that a whisper floating through them?

"Clay...Clay..."

I squinted into the shadows. "Aggie? Don't be scared. We'll sort this out."

Behind me, the floorboard creaked.

"Aggie?" I began to turn.

Something rammed my skull. Staggering, I reached for the wall. But it spun away from me like a Ferris wheel on steroids.

Smash. I got hit again. I glimpsed two golden specks of evening sun, then—

Blackout.

Chapter Six

"Clay, where are you?"

It was Bradley Costello's voice, faint and scared.

I struggled to open my eyelids. They were heavier than planet Earth. Just trying to open them sent pain shooting through my head.

I was slumped beside the locker. How did I get here? Trying to remember hurt.

Oh, yeah. Someone had slammed me.

I forced myself up. An object clanged from my hand to the ground. I squinted at it. A wrench. It multiplied into a dozen wrenches, doing a ring-around-the-rosy.

I heard footsteps, frantic, pounding. To the right of the tube, racing down the Boa stairs, was Judd.

It was Judd who'd bashed me on the head.

"*Clay!*" Panting, Brad scrambled up through the trees. He tried to hoist himself onto the platform, then fell back. I didn't care about Brad's dorkiness—I'd never been so glad to see anyone.

The second time, he managed it. He glanced around, glasses slipping off his nose. Then, spotting me, he ran over to help me up. "Say something, Clay."

Through leaden lips, I muttered, "Something, Clay."

"Don't joke," Brad gulped. "This is serious. Head injuries, left untreated, can result in death within twenty-four hours." Brad wiped his handkerchief over his face. "What happened? Where's Aggie?"

"Aggie?" I repeated stupidly.

Brad's face, blurring in and out of my vision, nodded. "I saw her on the launch platform. I knew Dad and Detective Mulligan wanted to talk to Aggie. I called the office, then hurried up here. I didn't think she could get away if you and I stopped her."

I leaned heavily on Brad's arm and we stood up. Blackness gathered in front of my eyes again. I fought the urge to pass out.

"I didn't see Aggie," I told Brad. "Just Judd."

Brad blinked owlishly at me. "I didn't see Judd. Just Aggie."

I groaned. This was turning into a brain-twister, and right now I didn't have a brain. Judd had knocked it out of my skull.

More footsteps pounded on the Boa stairs. Mr. Costello rushed up with a pudgy man in a shiny gray suit.

"Dad! Detective Mulligan!" Brad shouted. "My friend is badly injured!"

My friend. I didn't deserve that, after all the times I'd shrugged Brad off.

Mr. Costello jabbed 9-1-1 into his cell phone. "We'll get you help, Clay."

Detective Mulligan shoved his angry face into mine. "Where's Agatha Wentworth, mister? What did you do with her?"

I stretched one arm over Brad's shoulders, one over his dad's. The Costellos bore me down the stairs toward the platform—and the ambulance waiting beside it.

Detective Mulligan puffed alongside us. "C'mon, Clay. You're Aggie's boyfriend. People saw you together all the time. *Where is Aggie? Where's the missing dough?"*

I could hardly hear him. Then I realized why. Inside the tube, water was surging again.

But that didn't make sense. Brad had switched it off.

Mulligan was still badgering me. "Tell me what you did with the forty grand."

Bile rose in my throat. I spat it out, not too far from Mulligan's face. "You need to talk to Judd, not me."

"We *are* talking to Judd," the detective assured me. "He's at the base of the Boa, answering questions. Like you should be."

At the base of the Boa. Then it was Judd who'd turned the water back on.

Why?

"Leave Clay alone," Mr. Costello barked at Mulligan. "Can't you see what condition he's in? Try being human, Detective."

We reached the base of the Boa. Red with the effort of jogging, Detective Mulligan loosened his already crooked tie. Pulling a lollipop out of his pocket, he twisted the wrapper off. He dropped the wrapper carelessly on the ground. Chomping on the lollipop, he leered at Mr. Costello.

"Cops aren't paid to be human."

I stared at the landing pool. It was empty.

Blinking sweat out of my eyes, I looked up at the Boa's mouth. The door was shut. But that wasn't right, with the water running. If the water built up against a closed door, the tube would blow.

I tried to warn Mr. Costello, but I couldn't form the words.

Medics rushed up to us with a stretcher. I wanted to collapse on it. One of the medics asked my name. He was checking just how badly my skull had been bashed.

"Clay Gibson."

"Good boy."

Yeah, right. I'm a real mental champion.

The medics eased me onto the stretcher. I resisted. Trying to speak, I coughed out more bile.

"It's okay, Clay," Brad said.

He and Mr. Costello hadn't noticed the closed tube door. They were too busy worrying about me.

I couldn't talk, but I could move. Just.

Pushing the medics away, I staggered up the pool steps—and collapsed.

The Costellos' gazes followed me. They saw the closed door. Brad raced past me, grabbing the tube door's heavy metal latch. Mr. Costello joined him.

More people rushed up to help Brad and Costello. The pressure from the other side was sucking the door in, resisting them.

Then—a grotesque gurgling burst from the Boa.

The door crashed open. Brad and Mr. Costello leaped back. Water exploded out.

In a mighty wave, the Boa spewed Aggie Wentworth's body into the landing pool.

Chapter Seven

Aggie was pleading with me. Her eyes bulged out even more than usual from her pale face. "Why won't you listen? I try to talk to you about Lynx, and you just lose your temper."

The image rearranged itself. It wasn't Aggie's face I saw, but Brad's.

I was in a hospital bed with a bandage around my head and an intravenous tube in my arm. Brad was sitting in a chair beside me.

A nurse strode up. "You look upset," she said. To Brad she snapped, "What did you say to him?"

"I—I didn't say anything. Clay was sleeping, and…" Brad's Adam's apple bobbed nervously.

"He didn't do anything," I assured the nurse. Poor Brad. It was almost funny the way people always thought the worst of him. "I had a nightmare. How did I get here?"

"You're in Lions Gate Hospital. You passed out," Brad said. "Once Aggie's body appeared…" Unable to go on, Brad fiddled with the hem of his jacket.

The nurse told me briskly, "We'll switch your sleeping pills. Can't have nightmares, can we?"

I glared back. I didn't like being talked to like I was two.

"I don't want any drugs," I retorted.

I didn't believe in drugs. If I had a headache, I went for a swim. Water cleared everything away, leaving just freedom of movement.

The nurse's smile faded. "I see. A *macho* type."

"No," I said. More than ever, I wished I was swimming. I hated being confined. My coach once told me that a lot of athletes have claustrophobia.

The nurse was writing something on a chart. I had a feeling it wasn't a Mr. Congeniality nomination. Glancing at me with a smug, you're-in-my-power gleam, she marched off, the rubber soles of her shoes squeaking on the linoleum.

Brad looked half-embarrassed, half-admiring. "The way you stand up to people, Clay. I wish I could do that."

I thought of my infamous temper. "I doubt I'm an ideal role model."

Brad nodded toward a vase of sunflowers. "Your mom brought you those.

She and your dad will be pleased to know you're awake. I'm glad too. I was worried."

I managed a grin. The guy was all right.

Water came into my thoughts again, but now Aggie's pale face was superimposed on it. For Aggie, water hadn't meant freedom. It had been a death trap.

I struggled to a sitting position. "Tell me about Aggie. How'd she get caught in the Boa?"

Brad grew uncomfortable. I guessed he'd been told not to talk to me about Aggie. That's what the nurse had meant: *What did you say to upset him?*

"Tell me," I said.

Brad glanced around. Pulling the chair closer, he whispered, "I overheard the police talking to Dad. They said Aggie had a head injury, like yours. The cops figure someone knocked her unconscious, then stuffed her into the Boa."

He hesitated, fumbling with his tie.

"Tell me."

"They think the someone was you."

The room spun away from me.

"Clay." Brad was beside me, gripping my shoulders.

Slowly the room settled into place. I heaved deep breaths. "Judd killed Aggie," I choked out.

I remembered Judd getting the phone call from Aggie. He'd hurried back up the mountain to meet her. Spying me, he'd slammed my skull. The wrench I'd been clutching when I came to—I bet he'd used that.

I didn't remember how I'd got hold of the wrench. Maybe I'd forced it away from him in a struggle.

I mumbled out my theory to Brad. "And then Judd found Aggie—she was hiding in the forest, I'm sure of it. Judd bashed Aggie on the head and dragged her inside the Boa. After that…"

After that, Judd had hurried down to the control room and yanked the water wheel to full blast.

I would have told Brad this too, except the blackness was filling my brain again.

"Not feeling well?"

Detective Mulligan was leaning against the door frame, watching me with expressionless eyes.

I gripped the sheets to stop myself from snarling a reply. *Was I not feeling well?* What an idiot. But I needed to rein in my temper.

"Judd Wickstrom killed Aggie," I informed him. "You should arrest him."

Instead of hanging around here for no reason.

Mulligan shuffled toward the end of the bed. "Know what I think?"

Before I could stop myself, I shot back, "Enough to fit inside a golf ball?"

Mistake. The detective's expression stayed neutral, but he was white-knuckling the bed frame. Maybe he had a temper too. He said, "I think you killed Aggie because she was feeling guilty. She was threatening to blab.

"You went at her with a wrench. The two of you struggled for it. Aggie got in a blow before you clubbed her unconscious. Then you forced her into the waterslide, knowing she would drown as she was swept down the tube."

For a surreal moment, I could only gape. Mulligan's theory of the murder matched mine exactly—except it starred the wrong guy. I wanted to punch that sneer off his face. "I never struggled with Aggie. I didn't even see her. Judd had knocked me out with the wrench." I shrugged wearily.

Brad thought I was having another dizziness attack. "Put your head down," he said. "Shut your eyes and take deep breaths. It's the number-one way to fight off nausea."

Brad and his factoids, I thought. Even in my fury at Detective Mulligan, I felt the urge to laugh.

That saved me from reaching over, grabbing the lollipop Mulligan had started crunching on and shoving it down his throat.

Mulligan reminded me, "You, not Judd, were the one hanging out with Aggie. Everyone could see that you were her boyfriend. Everyone knew about your temper. They saw you, not Judd, knock her to the ground."

"No," I said. "*No.*"

My head was clearing. A realization was coming to light—not a pleasant one.

Aggie had glommed on to me from day one at Safari Splash. She was all over me at every opportunity, making sure everyone saw. She'd deliberately created a spectacle by falling down on the landing platform. I *knew* I hadn't pushed her hard.

I'd been bothered by Aggie's attention, because I hadn't encouraged her. I'd thought she was a nutter.

But she wasn't. She was following a plan.

"I was set up," I told Detective Mulligan. "It was very clever, if you think about it. Aggie was *performing* the whole time. Putting on an act. By glomming on to me, she was distracting attention from her real accomplice. Judd."

Chapter Eight

Mulligan straightened up and gaped at me. I thought I might have got past those hostile narrowed eyes, to his brain.

Then he laughed without humor. "Yeah, and how did that help Aggie? She's *dead*." He unwrapped another lollipop.

I shook my head. I was pretty sure Aggie's death wasn't part of Judd's plan. It had been a panicked decision.

But I couldn't prove it. Not while I was stuck here.

Mulligan's eyes bored into me like bullets. "You're lying."

"Clay doesn't lie," Brad objected. "Tell him about the Lynx, Clay."

I nodded. "Aggie was afraid of Judd. She called him 'the Lynx.' That's how he saw himself: preying on people and controlling them. Judd was also bullying Brad. He'd jump out of nowhere and scare Brad with this ghoulish lynx mask."

Detective Mulligan jammed the lollipop in his mouth and smiled unpleasantly. "Yeah, and who else is involved in this? Batman?"

"Don't make fun of Clay." Brad's voice shook. The detective was yet another bully he had to contend with. But Brad was standing up to him. "Clay and I both saw Judd wearing the mask."

The nurse bustled back in. This time I was glad to see her. "Stop upsetting my patient," she scolded Mulligan.

Mulligan started to retort but thought better of it. He wagged the lollipop at me. "Get some sleep for now, Gibson. I'll be back."

The nurse gave me two pills and a small plastic cup of water. "Take these. They'll help you sleep. What was with that detective—what's his name? *Bull*igan?"

I grinned wanly. "Mulligan. But you're not far off." I regretted my rudeness with her earlier. She was just doing her job.

Brad was hovering nearby, twisting the hem of his jacket. The nurse raised her eyebrows at him. "Maybe you need a sedative too, young man."

Brad goggled at her. "But sedatives are already overprescribed in our society, ma'am. According to a recent study—"

"Don't stay long," the nurse interrupted. "Rest, lots of it, is the best cure for Clay." She held up a hand to stop Brad quoting any more research as she left the room.

Once the squeak of her shoes faded down the hallway, I took the pills out from under my tongue. I dropped them into the vase of sunflowers by my bed.

Brad's eyes widened behind his glasses. "Hey, what are you doing? She said—"

"I know what she said." Pulling the tape off the intravenous tube, I eased the needle out of my arm. "I gotta get out of here. I need to find Judd and clear my name."

"But you're injured. If someone sees you…"

I stood up. Right away I felt dizzy. Grabbing Brad's arm for support, I said,

"I have nothing to lose, Brad. I'm on a fast slide to having my life destroyed. You gotta help me."

Minutes later Brad was wearing my hospital gown, and I was decked out in his white silk shirt and powder blue dress pants. He was taller than I was, so the shirtsleeves and pant legs were too long.

Brad pulled his jacket on over the hospital gown. He hugged it round himself to stop his nervous shivering. "If I'm caught, I'll get it from Dad big-time," he mourned. Sticking a hand in one pocket, he fiddled with coins. *Ka-ching, ka-ching.*

This reminded me of what Mr. Costello had said: *Their screams are my ka-chings.* I wondered how many ka-chings he'd get with the shadow of murder hanging over Safari Splash.

I told Brad, "Maybe I should just sneak out without getting you involved."

Brad heaved a deep breath and shook his head. "There's no way you can walk out of here in this"—he fingered the gown distastefully—"without attracting attention. Your own clothes were all bloodied. The police took them for evidence. No, Clay. You take my duds. You're my friend, and I want to help you."

You're my friend. Like I'd been any kind of friend to him over the years.

"My mom will come by soon," I said. "She'll bring me fresh clothes. Put them on, tell her what happened, and get the heck out. With any luck, Mom will show up before Mulligan comes back."

With any luck. Luck had been in short supply for me today.

Brad rattled the coins around in his pocket and looked doubtful.

As I slipped out, he was sliding under the bedcovers, pulling them over his head. The old ostrich routine…

I headed to the nearest elevator. I frowned as if I was thinking deep medical thoughts and couldn't possibly be on the run. Every few steps I felt dizzy and had to lean against a wall to steady myself.

In the elevator, I pushed back the too-long shirtsleeves and punched *G* for ground level.

Before the doors closed, an old woman hobbled in, helped by a nurse. The old lady did a double take. "My, my! What happened to your head?"

I'd forgotten about the bandage. The nurse stared. "A minor accident," I said. But even from the blurry reflection in the elevator's steel doors, I could tell my complexion was sickly.

"Pardon, sonny?" The old woman pushed her hearing aids in tighter.

The doors opened to the lobby. It was round, with shops and a food fair at the center, and halls branching off like spokes.

Detective Mulligan stomped along one of the halls yelling into his cell phone. "Whaddya mean, he *left*? Didn't anyone stop him?"

Somebody had already spotted Brad. The nurse, I thought. She'd come back to check on me.

"You don't look too well," the old woman said, squinting up into my face.

Mulligan was rasping, "C'mon, the kid has a head injury! It can't be that hard to find him."

With her hearing problems, the old woman was oblivious. But the nurse gave my bandage a sharp look.

The lobby was a sea of red and white uniforms. Candy stripers were listening to a woman explain volunteer duties. "You'll be asked to read aloud to elderly folks," she told the kids brightly.

I'd be asked to wear a pair of handcuffs, if I didn't watch it. Mulligan was headed toward the elevators. I had to get out of sight. I ducked behind the candy stripers and into the nearest shop, Lions Gate Boutique. I grabbed a smiley-face shirt off a rack and barreled into the change room. "Be right out," I called.

"But that's a woman's T-shirt…," the clerk objected.

"It's for my mom. I'm trying it on for her."

Great. I was as subtle as a tarantula in a bowl of vanilla pudding.

I opened the change-room door a crack. I was watching for Mulligan to disappear into an elevator.

I wasn't so lucky. After jabbing repeatedly on an elevator button, the detective's gaze turned sideways— to Janice Costello, who was walking by.

"Hey, missy," he yelled, so loudly the whole pack of candy stripers turned to stare. "You seen Clay Gibson?"

Janice wound her long hair around a wrist and regarded him coolly. "My name's Janice, not Missy. And I haven't seen Clay since yesterday, before he got attacked. I was just coming to visit him now."

Mulligan snorted. "Well, he's bolted, *Janice*." He pronounced her name with mock care. "Your buddy won't get far though. Not with that head injury."

In the boutique, I could see the clerk turn to frown at the change-room door.

Chapter Nine

Mulligan whipped out a fresh lollipop. Crunching into it, he barked at Janice, "We'll have your guy back upstairs in minutes—and this time we'll chain him down."

The elevator arrived, and he stomped inside.

Before the clerk could glance my way again, Janice walked into Lions

Gate Boutique. She was blushing from the stares of the candy stripers.

"I need a gift for a patient," she said.

The clerk nodded. "What kind of patient? Old, young, male, female?"

"Young. Male."

"We got a nice selection of Ts." The cashier waggled blue-painted fingernails at the racks lining the shop. "All colors. Whazz your boyfriend look like?"

Janice's blush went into overtime. I grinned in spite of myself.

"He's not my boyfriend. He has black hair, blue eyes."

"Oooo. A hottie." The clerk showed her a black T-shirt with two lions roaring by a gate.

"Lions…and a gate. Uh, cute," Janice said.

I had to get out of the boutique. Mulligan could come rampaging down to the lobby again at any minute.

"Maybe your boyfriend would prefer something sparkly." With another blue-nailed gesture, the clerk indicated a T-shirt with the hospital depicted in rhinestones.

I pushed the change-room door wide open. "I'm not the rhinestone type," I told the clerk.

I pulled Janice inside the change room.

"Hey, wait a sec," the clerk objected. "You can't—"

I shut the door.

Janice started to laugh, then whispered, "Are you out of your *mind*, Clay? That detective is after you."

"He's wrong, Janice. He thinks that I'm mixed up in the robbery—that I killed Aggie. But I *didn't*."

"I know you didn't. You couldn't." Her eyes were solemn. And green as ever.

I grinned at her. She almost grinned back. But then a frown took over. "You can't resolve this on your own, Clay. You should let the police figure it out."

"There's no point, Janice. Mulligan's already sentenced me to a lifetime of making license plates. Judd's the one Mulligan wants. I have to find him. Is he at work?"

"Safari Splash is closed," Janice said glumly. "Police orders, while they search for evidence. Judd's probably at home."

"Counting his forty grand in peace," I said bitterly. "Do you have access to employee files? Could you get me Judd's phone number?"

Janice bit her lip and nodded. "Yeah, I'll do that for you. I want to help you, and I know Brad would want me to."

I cracked open the change-room door. Except for the clerk, who was scowling at me, the shop was empty. "Okay, let's get outta here. By now Mulligan knows Brad switched places with me. It's a fair guess that he's ready to detonate."

"You mean—" Janice noticed my Brad outfit, and this time she did laugh. "You look ridiculous!"

"Thanks, Janice. I needed that vote of confidence."

I didn't want more people gawking at my bandaged head, so I grabbed an extra large ballcap. The still-amused Janice offered to pay for it, but I'd already pulled out my wallet.

Wait. I stared at it. This wasn't my wallet. It was Brad's. He'd left it in the pants pocket. My wallet was with my clothes—in police custody. Great. All my ID was in there.

I pulled bills and change from Brad's wallet to pay for the ballcap. I'd pay him back later.

Photos crammed the Costellos' den. There was Mr. Costello as a kid with swimming trophies, Mr. and Mrs. Costello's wedding, Janice and Brad.

"Brad always dresses better than me," Janice said over my shoulder. There was a fond note to her voice.

We'd gone to the Costellos' house to get the information on Judd. The Safari Splash office would be too risky.

Janice logged on to her dad's computer. I waited in the hall, where a full-length mirror showed me how dumb I looked with the shirtsleeves flapping around my wrist. I tried buttoning them, but they were still too baggy. In the end I just rolled them up.

Mrs. Costello was in the living room, sobbing into the phone. "How could Bill be so careless, leaving all that money in the till? Oh, Auntie Fran!"

Janice's mom hadn't noticed us come in. I hoped to keep it that way.

I edged past the living room. An especially tidy room caught my attention. No, it was more than tidy. It was *military*. On the dresser a brush, comb, suntan lotion and walnut box were lined up in perfect formation. In the closet, the clothes were grouped by color.

I grinned. This had to be Brad's room.

Janice was still busy. I wandered in.

Even a jeans-and-T-shirt guy like me could appreciate the wardrobe. Silk suits in every shade.

I stepped over to the dresser. The walnut box was polished so you could see every grain of the wood. I bet Brad had made this in shop. I'd made a similar one at my school. Mine, which I'd given to my mom, was nowhere near as perfect as this.

I lifted the lid. The black-velvet-lined compartments glistened with gold jewelry: tie studs, cuff links, signet rings. All the compartments were full but one.

Brad sure liked his finery. The bling was nice enough, but I was more interested in the box's craftsmanship. Brad had really worked on this. A labor of love.

Janice stood, slightly breathless, in the doorway. She waved a piece of paper. "I found Judd's cell number. I hope you know what you're doing, Clay."

"Janice?" It was Mrs. Costello's voice. "Is that you, dear?"

We gawked at each other. Uh-oh.

Janice's brain shifted into gear first. She whispered, "There's a phone in my parents' room. Call Judd from there and leave through the patio doors. I'll meet you at the bus stop in ten." She hurried off to greet Mrs. Costello in a cheery voice.

It bugged me that Janice had to deceive her mom. And that I had to hide from the law. Judd had set me up. *They toy with their prey before devouring it.* I gripped the lid of the walnut box to keep from slamming it down in frustration.

My mind went back to the moment I'd found the mask, before Judd snuck up behind me and bashed me with the wrench. That was the moment everything went black.

The darkness seeped into my brain now. The room spun. I had to stay conscious. I had to keep the darkness away. I took deep breaths and focused on the bling, all the bright gold inside the walnut box.

Slowly the darkness drew back. Then it vanished. My vision cleared.

And, suddenly, so did my memory. I remembered exactly what had happened at the top of the Boa. The memory stunned me, but it calmed me too.

Now I had all the information I needed. And it was 100 proof. With it, I could get whatever I wanted.

I punched in Judd's cell number.

"Yeah," said Judd.

Did I imagine the smugness in his voice—the assurance that he'd gotten away with a crime?

"It's Clay," I said.

There was silence on the other end. I plowed into it. "I want in on the forty grand."

Chapter Ten

Janice and I hurried up the dirt road to the side entrance of Safari Splash. It was a steep road through the forest—and a lonely one. The police had blocked off the entrance to the road. No trucks rumbled in with supplies, and no employees were driving in for shifts.

Safari Splash looked like a ghost town. Well, ghost *jungle*. The huge, painted faces of the animals, fun when the rides were operating, seemed garish with no water gushing around them.

Janice swiped her employee card through the gate's sensor. The lock clicked open.

Before Janice could say anything, I grabbed the card out of her hand, pushed through the gate and shut it again.

Bewildered, she stared through the chain links at me. The plan we'd agreed on was that she'd come with me. I'd meet Judd at the base of the Boa. Janice would wait around the corner and listen. She'd hear his admission of guilt. She'd be my witness.

I'd never intended to stick to the plan.

I leaned heavily against the gate. I felt sick from rushing around in this heat, sicker about lying to Janice.

I closed my eyes for a moment.

"Clay, what's happening?" Janice's face was puzzled, not angry. She still trusted me. I forced myself to look at her. I'd never liked a girl, all at once, *wham*, like this before. She liked me too. I was sure of it.

And I was about to throw it all away.

"Hey," I said gently. "It's better I go on my own. I'm sorry."

Janice shook her head, confused. "You can't do this by yourself. Not in your condition."

I couldn't possibly justify what I was about to do, so I didn't speak.

Janice hesitated, then reached up to touch my hand through the fence. She thought I was being noble. If she only knew.

"Clay," she began.

Withdrawing my hand, I turned and walked into the water park.

I had told Judd I wanted to meet at the top of the waterslide—for old times' sake,

I'd added as a joke. He hadn't laughed at that. But then I hadn't either.

I'd also told Judd what I knew. This info, if shared with the cops, would clinch his arrest. Judd had to agree to my demands.

Gripping the rail, I started climbing the Boa steps. Whatever happened, this would be my last visit to Safari Splash. Mr. Costello wouldn't have me back after this.

As much as I hadn't wanted to work here, I was sorry. I'd miss the challenges, even the barfing and complaining. Mom had been right. I had learned to be more tolerant.

The top of the Boa was quiet, except for the rustle of trees and the beep-like chirping of chickadees. The launch pool was empty. With no customers, there was no point in turning the water on.

I eased into the pool and sat on the edge of the Boa tube. My bandage was making me itchy, so I peeled it off.

I realized the chickadee beeps had stopped.

Someone was in the forest, just beyond the platform. Someone as quiet and stealthy as a lynx.

I felt eyes on me, studying, calculating.

Janice's words haunted me. *You can't confront Judd on your own*.

But I wanted this confrontation. I was tired of being toyed with.

I shifted back into the tube, trying to get out of the sun's rays. I heard the crackle of a twig snapping underfoot.

He was approaching.

There was a rustle as he pushed past a fir tree. He swung himself up on the platform. He slipped and almost fell back.

But then Bradley Costello always had been clumsy.

Chapter Eleven

Straightening, Brad brushed his clothes. Under his powder blue jacket, he wore a ripped T-shirt and too-short jeans.

He explained, "Your mom gave me the change of clothes she'd brought for you." Brad glanced down at the less-than-fashionable clothes with distaste. "I didn't have time to go home. First that cop grilled me, then Judd called."

Brad peered at me curiously. "I was surprised. I didn't think you were bright enough to figure out that I'm Lynx. Well, not *L-Y-N-X*—"

"No," I cut him off. "Though you did your best to make me think so."

Brad jumped down into the empty pool. He didn't speak. He just stared at me through those thick glasses.

The forest was silent. It was early afternoon, so the sun was pouring down Grouse Mountain. It had been different yesterday. When I was slammed on the head, the sun was too low to blitz the mountain. Grouse had been pretty much in shadow.

The two bright spots I had seen as I fell couldn't have been sunlight. I had assumed they were, till the moment in Brad's room, when I looked inside the walnut box.

When I saw the velvet-lined compartments, filled with gold jewelry.

Except for one compartment. One was missing bling.

It was missing cuff links—*the two bright spots had shone off my attacker's sleeves*.

And then I'd known my attacker was Brad.

At the hospital, I'd assumed Brad was jingling loose coins. But later, when I pulled out his wallet in the hospital souvenir shop, it held his bills and change.

More important, it held his ID. I felt empty without my wallet. *But Brad had been too busy hiding the cuff links to remember his*.

When we switched outfits in the hospital, he'd dumped the cuff links from his shirt into his jacket pocket. That was why he hadn't let me wear the jacket. He'd been nervously clinking the cuff links together, not coins.

And earlier that day, after Brad fell into the pool, he hadn't removed his jacket even though it was sopping. He'd been afraid I'd see the links and make the connection.

"How did you get to be called 'Links'?" I asked.

"At school the three of us hung out together. Aggie, Judd and me—the outcasts," said Brad. "Aggie called me Links because at lunchtime I would polish my cuff links."

I noticed Brad's hands. I hadn't realized before how big-knuckled they were, with long, strong fingers.

I forced my gaze away from them, up to his face. "You gotta get some help. What you did was…"

I remembered Aggie's pale, lifeless face; the wet, limp yellow hair straggling down like mop ends. I turned away from Brad, not wanting to look at him.

I blurted out loudly, accusingly, "Why did you do it, Brad? Why did you steal from your Dad? *Why did you kill Aggie Wentworth?*"

Brad sat down on the edge of the tube. He began to speak, choked, then tried again. "All my life, I've heard nothing but *Clay this, Clay that*. What a great athlete you are. How much you were like Dad. And all the time you wouldn't give me the time of day."

I was sweating. I backed farther into the shade of the Boa tube. It was flat for the first twelve yards, before the first plunge.

Brad raised his voice so I would still hear him. "When Dad hired you, I decided I would find a way to make you pay. I got Aggie and Judd jobs at the water park. Dad was pleased that I was making friends.

"When I realized that Dad left money in that till drawer all week, the robbery became a cinch. Aggie would steal the forty grand and we'd split it. *We'd set you up to take the blame*. You wouldn't seem so wonderful then!" Brad gave a shrill laugh.

"Aggie would glue herself to you. Everyone at the water park would assume you were girlfriend-boyfriend. She'd claim you sweet-talked the PIN out of her. Judd would say he saw the money in your knapsack."

Brad's shoulders sagged. "But then Aggie started liking you, just like everyone does. She told me she couldn't go through with it.

"During her fight with Judd, when she begged him to confess to Dad, I was behind the bamboo screen. I called her back there. I tried to talk her into staying with the game plan.

"She got mad and tried to leave. I grabbed her, begged her to listen. She pulled away—and fell, smashing her head against the corner of the freezer.

"She was *dead*." Tears trickled from under Brad's glasses. He removed them and wiped at the tears with the back of his hand. "I was scared. I didn't know what to do. I hid her body in the freezer."

I remembered stepping behind the bamboo screen. I remembered my certainty that Aggie was nearby. She'd been nearby, all right. Who knew? Maybe the dead made their presence felt. Maybe Aggie's ghost had lingered, trying to warn me. *Watch out, Clay...*

Aggie's face floated into my vision. The image was too vivid. I was fever-hallucinating. I shook my head to get her out of the way.

Brad heaved a deep breath. He put his glasses back on. "The only way out was to frame you for Aggie's death too. I counted on your flaw, Clay. Your explosive temper. People had seen you push Aggie around.

"When you went to look for the mask, I phoned Judd. I told him you might be listening, so he should act like it was Aggie on the phone. I wanted you to think she was at the top—alive. I snuck up behind you on the platform and bashed you with that wrench. I put the wrench into your hand so you'd get blamed for hitting Aggie.

"I shoved Aggie's body into the tube. I called Judd and got him to turn the water on full blast. The frame-up was complete."

I said slowly, "You may not have meant to kill Aggie, but you did plan the robbery. Not for money though. For revenge—against me."

A small smile flickered on Brad's face. "Yeah. You got it, Clay. I was going to savor seeing the guy Dad idolized go down for the robbery. Now everyone will think you're a murderer too."

The painkillers were wearing off. My head was throbbing. I felt disgust—but also pity. Brad had been shut out by me, by his father, by almost everyone, all these years.

Brad said, "It's too bad that I can't enjoy all my hard work the way I wanted."

Hardly knowing what I was doing, I crawled deeper into the tunnel. "What do you mean, Brad?" I called back.

Brad stuck his head inside the Boa tunnel. He explained, as if he was sharing one of his factoids, "Because now I have to kill you."

Brad crawled after me into the Boa tube. I pressed up against the wall. Ordinarily I could have swabbed the tube floor with Brad, but in my condition I was no match for anyone. My only chance was to knock him sideways, then make it out to the forest.

As plans went, it was pretty lame.

As Brad advanced, I slid along the wall toward the tube opening. *Distract him. Get him to brag some more.* I said,

"You got Judd to put on a lynx mask and make it obvious to me that he was wearing it. What was that about?"

Brad checked his watch. "Aggie warned Judd she'd tell everything. She said she'd already mentioned 'Links' to you. She said next time she'd tell you who Links was.

"I had to convince you that it was an animal reference. After I went home to change my suit, I stopped by a costume shop for a lynx mask. I got Judd to wear it while I was visiting you. That way you'd think of lynxes—and you'd suspect him of being *the* Lynx.

"I fed you a line about being bullied. It was vital that you feel sorry for me, Clay."

I couldn't see straight. There were several Brads floating across my field of vision. I focused on the one in the middle. "I didn't feel sorry for you, Brad. I liked you. But know what? I feel *real* sorry for you now, buddy."

Brad didn't reply. Again he checked his watch. Brad—the many Brads in my vision—fished the cuff links out of his pocket. He rolled them around again like dice.

Maybe Brad was thinking about dice too. He shrugged, "You took a gamble, champ. And you lost."

The different Brads formed a circle and spun like a Ferris wheel. More than anything, I wanted to shut them out, to sleep. I leaned back and rested my eyes.

The first spray of water was refreshing, like rain.

But it wasn't rain. I struggled to sit up.

The few drops turned into a coursing river. Water was surging from the landing pool into the tube. It was now clear to me why Brad kept checking his watch.

He had set the timer in the control room to open the pipes. The Boa was filling. He'd set the controls to full blast.

Brad intended to drown me.

Chapter Twelve

I started sloshing toward the tube entrance, but Brad blocked me. "This is what I'm gonna tell them: You set the timer. You tried to shove me in to drown me. But I got away."

We both swayed in the force of the water. He said, "I made sure to shut the door at the end of the tube, Clay. And you won't be able to swim up again.

Being a champ won't help even you."

I dove for his legs, toppling him. I crawled toward the daylight-filled tube opening.

Brad dragged me back by the feet.

I was underwater now. Brad was above me, fist upraised for a punch that would knock me unconscious—like Aggie had been.

I veered sideways as his fist descended. I staggered up. By now Brad's wet glasses were blurring his vision. He flailed his arms wildly, unable to pinpoint me.

Still, if I tried to move past him, those flailing arms would lock on to me. There wasn't enough room in the tube to give him a wide berth.

I made a decision: if I was going to die, let it be by water, not Bradley Costello. I could at least die by something I'd always loved.

Brad lurched closer. The water was swirling around our waists now. I leaned back so I was floating. Lifting one foot, I smashed it into Brad's face.

I didn't need to backstroke away from him. The water carried me toward the first plunge in the waterslide. I saw Brad's glasses splinter—saw blood spurt from his nose.

And then I was swept down the tube.

The Boa's initial flat surface was fairly gentle. Now, with the gravity of that first drop, the current turned into a vortex. The Boa was sucking me down, whirling me around in a fury of bubbles and white foam.

It was a minute and a half to the bottom of the Boa. Holding my breath that long was nothing—as a swimmer, I was trained to hold it for at least two minutes.

Another challenge bothered me more: Boa's killer current. A strong swimmer might survive it. But I'd been battered and bashed around. Brad's words came back: *Being a champ won't help even you.*

No. I wouldn't think about that. I wouldn't waste energy on Brad's taunts. I had to survive second by second. I had to prepare for the Boa's first twist. I remembered hearing the echoes from rafts hitting the turns. A rubber raft could survive being hurled against a wall. I wasn't so sure about my damaged skull. I wrapped my arms over my head—

Wham. I took the first turn. My left shoulder crunched against the wall. I barely missed bashing my skull.

Down and down I went. The water was tossing me around. I was going to ram feet-first against the next turn. If that happened, I could break both legs.

I curled into a ball. *Smash.* I hit the turn sideways.

There was a long plunge here. I had a few seconds' break from worrying about the next turn. The drawback to falling straight was that I built up speed. I was really going to slam into the next turn.

The water cartwheeled me again. I was falling so fast, I was disoriented. I couldn't tell how I was going to hit the turn. I tightened my arms around my head and prayed—

BAM. BAM.

I collided against the wall so hard, I actually bounced and met it again. I heard my right arm crack and splinter. Pain seared it. I opened my mouth for an agonized yell that blew out in a hundred bubbles.

Forget swimming back up the tube once I reached the bottom. There was no way I'd manage that. My right arm was totaled.

But then, I didn't *need* to swim up the Boa again.

Because Brad was wrong about the door. The Boa barfed me out with a mega-splash into the landing pool.

One of my knees touched bottom. After what I'd been through, the bump was more like a caress. Unable to use my right arm, I flailed with the left and kicked clumsily upward. I had to fight against the water gushing out of the Boa. My lungs and ears felt ready to burst with the strain of holding my breath.

I swam upward at a diagonal to avoid the force of the downpour. I needed to reach the side of the pool...I needed to breathe...

By the side of the pool, the water was calmer. I could see the surface—and through it—to the huge Boa mouth leering down at me. I plowed up and felt air on my face.

I exhaled, then glugged oxygen back in. Propping my good arm over the side of the pool, I heaved breaths in and out.

No dessert was sweeter than this. Why had I never noticed how pure and fresh the air was around here?

I heard footsteps.

My first thought was: *Brad*.

But Brad couldn't have made it down the mountain this fast. Or could he? I wasn't sure how long I'd been hanging on to the side of the pool.

With an effort, I leaned my chin on my arm and looked up.

Detective Mulligan leered—not unlike the plastic Boa—down at me. "So, I get to make my arrest, after all."

I couldn't say anything. Couldn't speak.

The detective knelt. "Looks like you wrecked your arm pretty bad, son."

I glanced behind me. Blood was clouding the pool. I nodded. Then I shook my head. "I don't know anything anymore, sir. Do what you have to do."

"Oh, I will." Mulligan dragged me out of the pool. Removing a pair of handcuffs from a jacket pocket, he dangled them in front of me. In the slanting sun, they sparkled like Brad's cuff links.

"Detective! No!"

Janice was running toward us.

"Don't arrest Clay. He didn't kill Aggie—he didn't steal Dad's money. I'm sure of it!"

Mulligan rolled his eyes. "Young love. Give me a break."

Janice bounded up the stairs to the platform. She sat down and put her arms around me. "I'm so sorry, Clay. What happened? Did he do this to you?" She shot a foul look at Mulligan.

It should have been funny. Yeah, I'd laugh about this one day. When I was eighty.

But I could live to be a hundred, and Janice would never put her arms around me again.

Footsteps pounded down the stairs, interrupted by a crash and an *oof!* Brad tripped and fell as he hurried down. Typical Bradley klutziness. That should have been funny too.

Limping toward us, Brad shouted, "I'm so relieved you caught him, Detective. He tried to kill me up there. We struggled, and—"

"What are you saying, Brad?" Janice stared at him in disbelief.

Brad gulped and blurted, "Get away from Clay, Jan. He's a murderer."

"You don't need to say another word," Detective Mulligan assured Brad. He stepped forward with the handcuffs.

And, with a deft *click*, snapped them around Brad's wrists.

Brad turned a satisfying shade of purple. "Not *me*, Detective. Clay took the money.

Clay drowned Aggie. They were a couple. Everyone knew. And Judd saw Clay—"

"Weren't you listening, Costello?" barked Mulligan. "I don't need you to say anything. Because you've already told me all I need to know."

"Whaa—?" Brad gaped from the detective to me.

"Yeah, that's right, brainiac," Mulligan said. "I heard every word you said through the tube. You planned the robbery with Judd and Aggie. Only Aggie had second thoughts, and now she's dead.

"One of my officers is arresting Judd at his home right now. We're gonna book him as your accomplice."

Brad looked like he'd finally met the factoid he couldn't compute.

Mulligan smiled coolly at him. "Boa's famous for its echo effect, right?" He nodded toward me. "It was young Clay's idea. He phoned me, right after he phoned Judd. Said he was going to get a confession out of you at the top of the tube. The deal was, I'd wait at the bottom of the tube by the open door and listen."

Janice turned on me, green eyes fiery with accusation. "You set Brad up. *You set up my brother.*"

Brad was so stunned, he started rolling the cuff links around in one of his cuffed hands. He'd been holding them all the time.

I said wearily, "You were right, Brad. I did gamble. But you were the one who lost."

Chapter Thirteen

It was a week later. Safari Splash was still closed. No one was allowed in until the police finished their investigation. With no one around, animals—real animals—had ventured out of the forest. Raccoons ambled around the concession, looking for French fries. Squirrels raced up and down on top of the tubes.

Detective Mulligan and I stood at top of the Boa. It was my last visit to the water park. Mr. Costello didn't want an employee who'd betrayed his son.

"It all comes down to dirty laundry," I said.

Mulligan nodded. He unpeeled a lollipop and stuck it in his mouth. "Yup, the Costellos' dirty laundry is out in the open now. Bradley has serious emotional problems. It's better his family knows about them. Now Brad can get help. Let's hope he won't target any more victims like Aggie Wentworth."

A vision of Aggie's pleading face hovered in front of me.

I nodded. "That's all true, Detective. But I didn't mean *that* kind of dirty laundry."

I led him behind the bamboo screen to the hamper where attendants tossed used towels. Lifting the lid, I explained, "Before Brad sneaked up on me, I was holding the lynx mask—the one Judd had worn. Aware Judd would be back any minute, I stashed it. For a long time I couldn't remember where. Then I realized I'd hidden it where no one ever looks."

I pushed several towels aside, and there it was. The lynx mask.

"Perfect," said Mulligan. "So much for Judd's denials about being Brad's accomplice. Forensics will show he wore it." The detective pulled out a pair of plastic gloves and a plastic bag. With the gloves on, he took hold of the mask by the edge and dropped it into the bag.

"Yeah, sure," I said. "Everything's just perfect."

I was remembering how Janice had turned sharply away from me to climb into the police car with Brad. I had phoned her a few times, but she kept hanging up.

Mulligan clattered the lollipop around in his mouth. "Still thinking about the Costello girl?"

"She'll never forgive me."

The detective zip-sealed the plastic bag. "I dunno, kid. Never's a long time. I could see she liked you."

I looked at Mulligan. There was something in those narrowed eyes I hadn't seen before. A glint of kindness.

"I thought you said cops weren't human," I said.

"Did I?" He crunched down on his lollipop, releasing waves of grape scent. "Well, you better keep my secret then."

Melanie Jackson is the author of the popular Dinah Galloway Mystery series, as well as *The Big Dip* in the Orca Currents series. Melanie lives in Vancouver, British Columbia.

orca currents

For more information on all the books
in the Orca Currents series, please visit
www.orcabook.com.